I Know
My Husband Better!

by Elizabeth and Alex Lluch

WS Publishing Group
www.WSPublishingGroup.com
San Diego, California 92119

I Know My Husband Better!

Part of *The Husband & Wife Challenge*

By Elizabeth and Alex Lluch

Published by WS Publishing Group
San Diego, California 92119
Copyright © 2008 by WS Publishing Group

Designed/Illustrated by WS Publishing Group:
David Defenbaugh

For Inquiries:
Logon to www.WSPublishingGroup.com
E-mail info@WSPublishingGroup.com

ISBN 13: 978-1-934386-16-3

Printed in China

Contents

Introduction

Welcome to *The Husband & Wife Challenge*. Are you ready to bet that you know your husband better than he knows you? This entertaining game will help you learn things about each other that you didn't know or were afraid to ask.

How to play the game

First, fill out and sign the *Wife's Contract* on the following page.

Second, exchange books with your husband and fill out the *Husband's Answer Sheet* (located in the back of his book). Have your husband fill out the *Wife's Answer Sheet* (located in the back of this book). Once both of you have filled out your answer sheets, tear them from the books, keep them out of sight, and swap books again.

Third, to the best of your abilities, answer the 100 multiple-choice questions about your husband. Select the best answer for each question.

Fourth, exchange answer sheets with your husband and compare your answers.

Fifth, add up your scores. Each correct answer is worth one point. The person with the most points wins! The loser must provide the rewards checked off on the signed contract.

How well did you score?

90 and above	80 - 89	70 - 79	69 and below
Above and beyond most wives!	Typical wife.	Not bad for a wife.	You're just like a husband.

Wife's Contract

Place a check mark in the square next to the reward(s) that you are willing to provide if your husband wins the challenge. You can select one or more of our suggestions or add your own. To be fair, each of you must select the same number of rewards.

I hereby agree to perform the following in the event that my husband wins *The Husband & Wife Challenge*:

☐ Take him to his favorite restaurant

☐ Give him a new magazine each week for a month

☐ Give him a 30-minute body massage

☐ Wash his car

☐ Take him to a sporting event

☐ Take him to an electronics store

☐ Make him breakfast in bed

☐ Let him go on a guys' night out

☐ _____

_____   _____
Signature   Date

About Your Husband

1. What is his astrological sign?

   _____

2. He would describe himself as:
   a. __ The life of the party
   b. __ A go-getter
   c. __ Quiet and smart
   d. __ The last comic standing
   e. __ God's gift to women

3. His goal in life is to:
   a.__ Have a big family
   b.__ Rule the world
   c.__ Work as little as possible
   d.__ Make the world a better place
   e.__ Inherit his family's money

4. What does he worry about the most?
   a.__ His health
   b.__ His money
   c.__ His family
   d.__ Being a spokesman for Rogaine

5. His idea of a good time is:
   a.__ A candlelight dinner with you
   b.__ A guys' night out
   c.__ Work (he's a workaholic)
   d.__ Anything that involves sitting in front of a
        screen with beer and potato chips

Pop Culture

6. Which TV show does he like best?
   a.___ "Seinfeld"
   b.___ "Friends"
   c.___ "The Simpsons"
   d.___ "SpongeBob"

7. Which of these movies does he like best?
   a.___ *Gone With the Wind*
   b.___ *The Exorcist*
   c.___ *Star Wars*
   d.___ *Finding Nemo*
   e.___ *Die Hard*

8. If he could be any comic book superhero, which one would he be?
   a.___ Superman – his X-ray vision allows him to see through clothes
   b.___ Elastic Man – he can reach the beer in the fridge without leaving the couch
   c.___ Batman – he has the best gadgets and the coolest car
   d.___ Spiderman – he can catch you in his web

9. Which of these people would he like to meet most?
   a.___ Pamela Anderson
   b.___ Paris Hilton
   c.___ Angelina Jolie
   d.___ Rosie O'Donnell

Personality

10. He would most likely choose to be:
    - a.___ The President of the United States
    - b.___ The president of a Fortune 500 company
    - c.___ The president of a small business
    - d.___ A house-husband

11. Which of these personality types describes him the best?
    - a.___ Optimist
    - b.___ Pessimist
    - c.___ Realist
    - d.___ Free spirit

12. Which of these describes him the best?
    - a.___ Makes things happen
    - b.___ Watches things happen
    - c.___ Wonders what happened
    - d.___ Thinks nothing happened

13. Which does he appreciate the most about you?
    - a.___ Your honesty
    - b.___ Your sense of humor
    - c.___ Your kindness
    - d.___ Your money

14. He is most terrified of:
    - a.___ Heights
    - b.___ Creepy crawlies
    - c.___ Public speaking
    - d.___ Being polygraphed by your father

Talents

15. Which is he most talented at?
    - a.___ Playing an instrument
    - b.___ Drawing
    - c.___ Fixing things
    - d.___ Turning you on

16. Which of these does he do best?
    - a.___ Tune an engine
    - b.___ Play chess
    - c.___ Use a sewing machine
    - d.___ Bake a cake
    - e.___ Make you laugh

17. Which of these talents would he like to have the most?
    - a.___ Juggling
    - b.___ Doing magic tricks
    - c.___ Telling jokes
    - d.___ Burping the ABC's

18. What talent does he like most in a woman?
    - a.___ Cooking
    - b.___ Sewing
    - c.___ Cleaning
    - d.___ Dancing
    - e.___ Kissing

19. What type of woman does he prefer?
    - a.___ Intellectual
    - b.___ Athletic
    - c.___ Romantic
    - d.___ Nymphomaniac

Book Smarts

20. Which self-help book would he most likely read?
    a.__ *Simple Principles™ to Enjoy Life & Be Happy*
    b.__ *Simple Principles™ to Feel Better & Live Longer*
    c.__ *Simple Principles™ to Become a Millionaire*
    d.__ *Simple Principles™ to Satisfy Your Woman in Bed*

21. Which type of book does he like the most?
    a.__ Biographies
    b.__ How-to books
    c.__ Novels
    d.__ Comic books

22. What part of the newspaper does he read first?
    a.__ The front page
    b.__ Sports
    c.__ Weather
    d.__ Celebrity gossip

23. Which magazine does he like the most?
    a.__ *Popular Mechanics*
    b.__ *National Geographic*
    c.__ *People*
    d.__ *Men's Health*
    e.__ *Playboy*

24. Which kind of writing would he enjoy reading the most?
    a.__ Action
    b.__ Comedy
    c.__ Mystery
    d.__ Romance

Childhood

25. Who was his best childhood friend?

    _____

26. He was most likely to be grounded for:
    a.___ Poor grades
    b.___ Staying out past curfew
    c.___ Beating up his siblings
    d.___ Setting things on fire

27. Which of these games did he enjoy most as a child?
    a.___ Football
    b.___ Baseball
    c.___ Cops and robbers
    d.___ Board games
    e.___ Spin the Bottle

28. If he broke something in the house, he would:
    a.___ Tell his parents
    b.___ Try to glue it back together
    c.___ Blame a sibling
    d.___ Blame the cat

29. As a kid, he collected:
    a.___ Bugs
    b.___ Coins or stamps
    c.___ Baseball cards
    d.___ Detention notes

Work

30. What was his first job?

   _____

31. Where would he most likely invest his money?
    a.__ In the stock market
    b.__ In real estate
    c.__ In a small business
    d.__ In a vacation timeshare for you

32. How does he feel about his current job?
    a.__ He loves it and would do it for free
    b.__ It's nothing special, but the money is good
    c.__ He would change it if he could
    d.__ Where else can he check Myspace.com and
       get paid for it?

33. If he won $20 million, which of these jobs
    would he most likely choose to do?
    a.__ Teacher
    b.__ Artist
    c.__ Forest ranger
    d.__ Stockbroker
    e.__ None of the above – he would be a beach bum

Favorites

34. Which animal would he like the most as a pet?
    a.__ A cat – they're very independent
    b.__ A dog – they're man's best friend
    c.__ A snake – they're exotic and dangerous
    d.__ A stuffed bunny – they're good company in bed

35. Which flavor of ice cream does he like the most?
    a.__ Vanilla
    b.__ Chocolate
    c.__ Coffee
    d.__ Mint
    e.__ Anything, as long as it's not fat-free

36. Which soda does he like the most?
    a.__ Coca-Cola
    b.__ Pepsi
    c.__ 7-Up
    d.__ Dr. Pepper
    e.__ Any of the above, as long as there's rum in it

37. On Sunday during football season, he:
    a.__ Watches every single game
    b.__ Watches only his favorite team
    c.__ Only checks out the scores
    d.__ Wonders why anyone would watch football

38. His ideal car is anything that:
    a.__ Is fast and foreign
    b.__ Can run on alternative fuel
    c.__ Can crush another car
    d.__ Has four tires and a steering wheel

Preferences

39. Which sport would he prefer to participate in?
    a.___ Anything that causes bodily harm
    b.___ Anything that doesn't make him sweat or get dirty
    c.___ Anything that requires using only his thumbs
    d.___ Anything with cheerleaders

40. Which of these does he prefer to watch on television?
    a.___ Sports
    b.___ The news
    c.___ Sitcoms
    d.___ Reality TV
    e.___ Cartoons

41. Which of these outdoor activities does he prefer?
    a.___ Hiking
    b.___ Camping
    c.___ Fishing
    d.___ Hunting
    e.___ Skinny-dipping

42. Which of these indoor activities does he prefer?
    a.___ Reading
    b.___ Watching television
    c.___ Playing computer games
    d.___ Sleeping
    e.___ Showing off his birthday suit

Shopping

43. What does he do if he finds a flat-screen TV he likes?
    a.__ Buys it on impulse
    b.__ Compares its specifications with other models
    c.__ Waits until it goes on sale
    d.__ Buys it on the Internet

44. He would rather go shopping:
    a.__ With you
    b.__ Alone
    c.__ With his friends
    d.__ With someone else's credit card

45. What is most important for him when buying clothes?
    a.__ Price
    b.__ Quality
    c.__ Style

46. If you lose him at a mall you will most likely find him at:
    a.__ A discount store
    b.__ A specialty store
    c.__ A lingerie store
    d.__ The food court

47. What would he prefer to receive as a gift?
    a.__ A book
    b.__ A DVD
    c.__ A CD
    d.__ A video game
    e.__ A subscription to a magazine that he wasn't allowed to read when he was a boy

Appearance

48. He would most likely get a scar from:
    a.__ Trying to rescue an injured animal
    b.__ Trying to juggle knives
    c.__ A fight with an ex-girlfriend
    d.__ Trying to walk and chew gum at the same time

49. What would he change about his appearance?
    a.__ His eyes
    b.__ His nose
    c.__ His biceps
    d.__ His beer belly

50. What does he like the least about himself?
    a.__ His personality
    b.__ His physique
    c.__ His family
    d.__ Nothing – he's perfect

51. Which of these people would he want to look like?
    a.__ George Clooney
    b.__ Brad Pitt
    c.__ David Beckham
    d.__ Bono
    e.__ None – he just wants to make their kind of
    money

School Days

52. Which high school did he go to?

   _____

53. If he didn't do his homework, his excuse would be:
   a.___ The dog ate it
   b.___ There was a death in the family
   c.___ His mother threw it away by accident
   d.___ Doing homework is against his religion

54. Which class was he most likely to ditch?
   a.___ Math
   b.___ History
   c.___ Science
   d.___ English

55. Which class would he never miss at school?
   a.___ Math
   b.___ History
   c.___ Science
   d.___ English

56. He was most likely sent to the principal's office for:
   a.___ Beating someone up
   b.___ Sleeping during class
   c.___ Ditching class
   d.___ Flirting with the history teacher

57. Did he ever cheat on an exam?
   a.___ No
   b.___ Once, but he got caught
   c.___ Only when he was really desperate
   d.___ Every chance he got

Teenage Years

58. As a teenager, he was most likely known as a:
   a.___ Geek
   b.___ Jock
   c.___ Freak
   d.___ Ladies man

59. What is his favorite memory as a teenager?
   a.___ His first car
   b.___ His first girlfriend
   c.___ His senior prom
   d.___ Watching the cheerleaders jump up and down

60. Who was his biggest crush as a teenager?
   a.___ The captain of the cheerleading team
   b.___ The nerdy girl in science class
   c.___ The tough chick who dropped out of school
   d.___ Anyone who wore a skirt

61. As a teenager, which of these did he most likely do?
   a.___ Lie to his parents
   b.___ Shoplift
   c.___ Cheat on an exam
   d.___ Have multiple girlfriends
   e.___ All of the above

Family Matters

62. Does he love his mother more than he loves you?
    a.__ Yes, he'll always be a mama's boy
    b.__ Yes, but you're a close second
    c.__ He loves you both equally
    d.__ He loves you more but don't tell his mom

63. He thinks of his father as:
    a.__ His best friend
    b.__ A source of wisdom
    c.__ A drill sergeant
    d.__ An alien from another planet

64. His mother is more like:
    a.__ A talk-show host
    b.__ Betty Crocker
    c.__ The school nurse
    d.__ An undercover cop

Social Life

65. His ideal Friday night would be spent:
    a.__ Relaxing with you at home
    b.__ Watching sports on TV
    c.__ Going to the movies
    d.__ Doing anything that involves drinking

66. He would rather go out with:
    a.__ A small group of friends
    b.__ A large group of friends
    c.__ His family
    d.__ Anyone who will pick up the tab

67. He would most likely participate in:
    a.__ Group sports
    b.__ Individual sports
    c.__ Virtual sports
    d.__ Who cares about sports?

68. With his friends, he is more likely to:
    a.__ Be a couch potato
    b.__ Go white-water rafting
    c.__ Check out babes
    d.__ Wind up in jail

69. His friends often try to convince him to:
    a.__ Act his age
    b.__ Get a haircut
    c.__ Get a tattoo
    d.__ Lend them some money

Situations

70. When he is frustrated, he prefers that you:
    a.__ Leave him alone
    b.__Talk to him about the problem
    c.__ Do something to take his mind off the problem
    d.__ Smack him on the head

71. What would he say if you found lipstick on his shirt?
    a.__ "It's from my mom"
    b.__ "It's a borrowed shirt"
    c.__ "Some woman confused me for her boyfriend"
    d.__ Nothing – he'd forget how to speak English

72. What would he do if he won the lottery?
    a.__ Spend the money as fast as he could
    b.__ Buy a business
    c.__ Invest in the stock market
    d.__ Share it with his friends and family
    e.__ Move to the South Pacific and start a new life

73. What would he do if he got lost?
    a.__ Stop and ask for directions
    b.__ Buy a map and figure out where he is
    c.__ Keep driving until he finds what he's looking for
    d.__ Give up and go home

74. When he retires, he will most likely:
    a.__ Play golf
    b.__ Go fishing
    c.__ Travel
    d.__ He'll never retire – you need that paycheck

Food and Drinks

75. Which of the following does he prefer with his chips?
    a.__ Nacho cheese
    b.__ Salsa
    c.__ Guacamole
    d.__ All the above mixed together

76. Which of these pizzas does he like the best?
    a.__ Plain cheese
    b.__ Meat lover's
    c.__ Veggie
    d.__ All of the above – if it's digestible he'll eat it

77. How does he eat an Oreo cookie?
    a.__ Sticks the whole thing in his mouth
    b.__ Dunks it in milk, then eats it
    c.__ Twists it open, licks the cream, then eats the
        two cookie halves
    d.__ Licks the cream, then puts the cookie back in
        the bag

78. How does he like his steak?
    a.__ Well-done
    b.__ Medium
    c.__ Rare
    d.__ As big as possible

79. Which type of food is he most likely to cook?
    a.__ American
    b.__ French
    c.__ Italian
    d.__ Anything he can heat in the microwave

Travels & Adventures

80. His favorite place to vacation is:
    a.__ Hawaii – surf, sun and snorkeling
    b.__ Mexico – chips and margaritas
    c.__ Europe – museums, culture and art
    d.__ His backyard – as long as he's got beer

81. The main reason he likes to travel is:
    a.__ Learning about other cultures
    b.__ Relaxation
    c.__ Eating exotic foods
    d.__ To get away from his family

82. Which of these would he like to visit the most?
    a.__ The Great Wall of China
    b.__ The Egyptian pyramids
    c.__ The Grand Canyon
    d.__ Las Vegas – what happens in Vegas stays in Vegas

83. Which of these people from history would he most
    like to meet?
    a.__ Marilyn Monroe
    b.__ Princess Diana
    c.__ Mother Teresa
    d.__ The Wicked Witch of the West

84. If he could visit any historical period, which would it be?
    a.__ The Stone Age – when getting a woman was as
         easy as clubbing her over the head
    b.__ Medieval times – when men could eat like pigs
    c.__ The Sixties – peace, love and rock 'n' roll
    d.__ The Disco Era – he thinks he's John Travolta

Daily Routine

85. Which one of these describes him the best?
    a.__ He likes to go to bed early, get up late
    b.__ He likes to go to bed early, get up early
    c.__ He likes to go to bed late, get up late
    d.__ He likes to go to bed late, get up early

86. Which home chore would he rather do?
    a.__ Wash the dishes
    b.__ Vacuum the carpet
    c.__ Do the laundry
    d.__ Take out the trash

87. What is his worst habit?
    a.__ Smoking
    b.__ Drinking
    c.__ Forgetting names
    d.__ Leaving the toilet seat up

88. Which of these would he prefer to do on Sunday morning?
    a.__ Have breakfast in bed with you
    b.__ Get up and go for a run
    c.__ Read the newspaper
    d.__ Sleep until noon

89. What would he do with an extra hour in his day?
    a.__ Exercise
    b.__ Read
    c.__ Sleep
    d.__ Work
    e.__ Spend it with you

Has He Ever

90. Has he ever broken a bone?
    Yes___ No___

91. Has he ever had multiple girlfriends at the same time?
    Yes___ No___

92. Has he ever fallen asleep while driving?
    Yes___ No___

93. Has he ever been in a car accident?
    Yes___ No___

94. Has he ever spent a night in jail?
    Yes___ No___

95. Has he ever been featured in the local newspaper?
    Yes___ No___

96. Has he ever stolen something of value?
    Yes___ No___

97. Has he ever gone skinny-dipping?
    Yes___ No___

98. Has he ever cheated in a past relationship?
    Yes___ No___

99. Has he ever been in an ambulance?
    Yes___ No___

100. Has he ever been on TV?
     Yes___ No___

Husband's Answer Sheet

Wife: Before you answer the questions in this book have your husband fill out this answer sheet. After he is finished have him remove it from this book.

1) _____

2) a.___ b.___ c.___ d.___ e.___

3) a.___ b.___ c.___ d.___ e.___

4) a.___ b.___ c.___ d.___

5) a.___ b.___ c.___ d.___

6) a.___ b.___ c.___ d.___

7) a.___ b.___ c.___ d.___ e.___

8) a.___ b.___ c.___ d.___

9) a.___ b.___ c.___ d.___

10) a.___ b.___ c.___ d.___

11) a.___ b.___ c.___ d.___

12) a.___ b.___ c.___ d.___

13) a.___ b.___ c.___ d.___

14) a.___ b.___ c.___ d.___

15) a.___ b.___ c.___ d.___

16) a.___ b.___ c.___ d.___ e.___

17) a.___ b.___ c.___ d.___

18) a.___ b.___ c.___ d.___ e.___

19) a.___ b.___ c.___ d.___

20) a.___ b.___ c.___ d.___

21) a.___ b.___ c.___ d.___

22) a.___ b.___ c.___ d.___

23) a.___ b.___ c.___ d.___ e.___

24) a.___ b.___ c.___ d.___

25) _____

26) a.___ b.___ c.___ d.___

27) a.___ b.___ c.___ d.___ e.___

28) a.___ b.___ c.___ d.___

29) a.___ b.___ c.___ d.___

30) _____

31) a.___ b.___ c.___ d.___

32) a.___ b.___ c.___ d.___

33) a.___ b.___ c.___ d.___ e.___

34) a.___ b.___ c.___ d.___

35) a.___ b.___ c.___ d.___ e.___

36) a.___ b.___ c.___ d.___ e.___

37) a.___ b.___ c.___ d.___

38) a.___ b.___ c.___ d.___

39) a.___ b.___ c.___ d.___

40) a.___ b.___ c.___ d.___ e.___

41) a.___ b.___ c.___ d.___ e.___

42) a.___ b.___ c.___ d.___ e.___

43) a.___ b.___ c.___ d.___

44) a.___ b.___ c.___ d.___

45) a.___ b.___ c.___

46) a.___ b.___ c.___ d.___

47) a.___ b.___ c.___ d.___ e.___
48) a.___ b.___ c.___ d.___
49) a.___ b.___ c.___ d.___
50) a.___ b.___ c.___ d.___
51) a.___ b.___ c.___ d.___ e.___
52) _____
53) a.___ b.___ c.___ d.___
54) a.___ b.___ c.___ d.___
55) a.___ b.___ c.___ d.___
56) a.___ b.___ c.___ d.___
57) a.___ b.___ c.___ d.___
58) a.___ b.___ c.___ d.___
59) a.___ b.___ c.___ d.___
60) a.___ b.___ c.___ d.___
61) a.___ b.___ c.___ d.___ e.___
62) a.___ b.___ c.___ d.___
63) a.___ b.___ c.___ d.___
64) a.___ b.___ c.___ d.___
65) a.___ b.___ c.___ d.___
66) a.___ b.___ c.___ d.___
67) a.___ b.___ c.___ d.___
68) a.___ b.___ c.___ d.___
69) a.___ b.___ c.___ d.___
70) a.___ b.___ c.___ d.___
71) a.___ b.___ c.___ d.___
72) a.___ b.___ c.___ d.___ e.___
73) a.___ b.___ c.___ d.___
74) a.___ b.___ c.___ d.___

75) a.___ b.___ c.___ d.___
76) a.___ b.___ c.___ d.___
77) a.___ b.___ c.___ d.___
78) a.___ b.___ c.___ d.___
79) a.___ b.___ c.___ d.___
80) a.___ b.___ c.___ d.___
81) a.___ b.___ c.___ d.___
82) a.___ b.___ c.___ d.___
83) a.___ b.___ c.___ d.___
84) a.___ b.___ c.___ d.___
85) a.___ b.___ c.___ d.___
86) a.___ b.___ c.___ d.___
87) a.___ b.___ c.___ d.___
88) a.___ b.___ c.___ d.___
89) a.___ b.___ c.___ d.___ e.___
90) yes___ no___
91) yes___ no___
92) yes___ no___
93) yes___ no___
94) yes___ no___
95) yes___ no___
96) yes___ no___
97) yes___ no___
98) yes___ no___
99) yes___ no___
100) yes___ no___

I Know
My Wife Better!

by Elizabeth and Alex Lluch

WS Publishing Group
www.WSPublishingGroup.com

San Diego, California 92119

I Know My Wife Better!

Part of *The Husband & Wife Challenge*

By Elizabeth and Alex Lluch

Published by WS Publishing Group
San Diego, California 92119
Copyright © 2008 by WS Publishing Group

Designed/Illustrated by WS Publishing Group:
David Defenbaugh

For Inquiries:
Logon to www.WSPublishingGroup.com
E-mail info@WSPublishingGroup.com

ISBN 13: 978-1-934386-16-3

Printed in China

Contents

Introduction

Welcome to *The Husband & Wife Challenge*. Are you ready to bet that you know your wife better than she knows you? This entertaining game will help you learn things about each other that you didn't know or were afraid to ask.

How to play the game

First, fill out and sign the *Husband's Contract* on the following page.

Second, exchange books with your wife and fill out the *Husband's Answer Sheet* (located in the back of her book). Have your wife fill out the *Wife's Answer Sheet* (located in the back of this book). Once both of you have filled out your answer sheets, tear them from the books, keep them out of sight, and swap books again.

Third, to the best of your abilities, answer the 100 multiple-choice questions about your wife. Select the best answer for each question.

Fourth, exchange answer sheets with your wife and compare your answers.

Fifth, add up your scores. Each correct answer is worth one point. The person with the most points wins! The loser must provide the rewards checked off on the signed contract.

How well did you score?

90 and above	80 - 89	70 - 79	69 and below
Above and beyond most husbands!	Great for a husband!	Not bad for a husband.	Typical husband.

Husband's Contract

Place a check mark in the square next to the reward(s) that you are willing to provide if your wife wins the challenge. You can select one or more of our suggestions or add your own. To be fair, each of you must select the same number of rewards.

I hereby agree to perform the following in the event that my wife wins *The Husband & Wife Challenge*:

☐   Take her for a romantic night out

☐   Send her flowers each week for a month

☐   Give her a 30-minute body massage

☐   Wash her car

☐   Take her dancing

☐   Take her shopping at the mall

☐   Make her breakfast in bed

☐   Let her go on a ladies' night out

☐   _____

_____   _____

Signature   Date

About Your Wife

1. What is her astrological sign?

   _____

2. She would describe herself as:
   a. __ The life of the party
   b. __ A go-getter
   c. __ Quiet and smart
   d. __ The last comic standing
   e. __ God's gift to men

3. Her goal in life is to:
   a. __ Have a big family
   b. __ Rule the world
   c. __ Work as little as possible
   d. __ Make the world a better place
   e. __ Inherit her family's money

4. What does she worry about the most?
   a. __ Her health
   b. __ Her money
   c. __ Her family
   d. __ Missing out on the biggest sale of the year

5. Her idea of a good time is:
   a. __ A candlelight dinner with you
   b. __ A girls' night out
   c. __ Work (she's a workaholic)
   d. __ Going shopping

Pop Culture

6. Which TV show does she like best?
   a.__ "Seinfeld"
   b.__ "Friends"
   c.__ "General Hospital"
   d.__ "Dora the Explorer"

7. Which of these movies does she like best?
   a.__ *Gone With the Wind*
   b.__ *Scary Movie*
   c.__ *Titanic*
   d.__ *The Wedding Planner*
   e.__ *Finding Nemo*

8. If she could be any Barbie® doll, which one would she be?
   a.__ Glamour Girl Barbie®
   b.__ Volleyball Beach Barbie®
   c.__ Hard Rock Barbie®
   d.__ None of the above – she's more of a Bratz™ doll

9. Which of these people would she like to meet most?
   a.__ Brad Pitt
   b.__ George Clooney
   c.__ Justin Timberlake
   d.__ Dog the Bounty Hunter

Personality

10. She would most likely choose to be:
    a.__ The President of the United States
    b.__ The president of a Fortune 500 company
    c.__ The president of a small business
    d.__ A housewife

11. Which of these personality types describes her the best?
    a.__ Optimist
    b.__ Pessimist
    c.__ Realist
    d.__ Free spirit

12. Which of these describes her the best?
    a.__ Makes things happen
    b.__ Watches things happen
    c.__ Wonders what happened
    d.__ Thinks nothing happened

13. Which does she appreciate the most about you?
    a.__ Your honesty
    b.__ Your sense of humor
    c.__ Your kindness
    d.__ Your money

14. She is most terrified of:
    a.__ Heights
    b.__ Creepy crawlies
    c.__ Public speaking
    d.__ Breaking a fingernail

Talents

15. Which is she most talented at?
    a.___ Playing an instrument
    b.___ Drawing
    c.___ Dancing
    d.___ Turning you on

16. Which of these does she do best?
    a.___ Make you jealous
    b.___ Make you calm
    c.___ Make you excited
    d.___ Bake a cake
    e.___ Make you laugh

17. Which of these talents would she like to have the most?
    a.___ Cooking
    b.___ Sewing
    c.___ Singing
    d.___ Flirting

18. What trait does she like most in a man?
    a.___ Creativity
    b.___ Earning potential
    c.___ Cleanliness
    d.___ Dancing
    e.___ Kissing

19. What type of man does she prefer?
    a.___ Intellectual
    b.___ Athletic
    c.___ Romantic
    d.___ Sex maniac

Book Smarts

20. Which self-help book would she most likely read?
    a.__ *Simple Principles™ to Enjoy Life & Be Happy*
    b.__ *Simple Principles™ to Feel Better & Live Longer*
    c.__ *Simple Principles™ to Become a Millionaire*
    d.__ *Simple Principles™ to Satisfy Your Man in Bed*

21. Which type of book does she like the most?
    a.__ Biographies
    b.__ Self-help
    c.__ Novels
    d.__ Astrology

22. What part of the newspaper does she read first?
    a.__ The front page
    b.__ Weather
    c.__ Celebrity gossip
    d.__ Coupon section

23. Which magazine does she like the most?
    a.__ *Better Homes and Gardens*
    b.__ *Martha Stewart Living*
    c.__ *People*
    d.__ *Women's Health*
    e.__*Playgirl*

24. Which kind of writing would she enjoy reading the most?
    a.__ Drama
    b.__ Comedy
    c.__ Mystery
    d.__ Romance

Childhood

25. Who was her best childhood friend?

   _____

26. She was most likely to be grounded for:
    a.__ Poor grades
    b.__ Staying out past curfew
    c.__ Talking too long on the phone
    d.__ Sneaking out of the house

27. Which of these games did she enjoy most as a child?
    a.__ Jacks
    b.__ Hopscotch
    c.__ Jumping rope
    d.__ Go Fish
    e.__ Spin the Bottle

28. If she broke something in the house, she would:
    a.__ Tell her parents
    b.__ Try to glue it back together
    c.__ Blame a sibling
    d.__ Blame the cat

29. As a kid, she collected:
    a.__ Dolls
    b.__ Coins or stamps
    c.__ Stuffed animals
    d.__ Boyfriends

Work

30. What was her first job?

    _____

31. Where would she most likely invest her money:
    a.__ In the stock market
    b.__ In real estate
    c.__ In a vacation
    d.__ In a pair of high heels

32. How does she feel about her current job?
    a.__ She loves it and would do it for free
    b.__ It's nothing special, but the money is good
    c.__ She would change it if she could
    d.__ Where else can she check Myspace.com and
       get paid for it?

33. If she won $20 million, which of these jobs
    would she most likely choose to do?
    a.__ Teacher
    b.__ Fashion designer
    c.__ Model
    d.__ Hairdresser
    e.__ Shopper – shop until she drops

Favorites

34. Which animal would she like the most as a pet?
    - a.___ A cat – they're very independent
    - b.___ A dog – one that will fit in her purse
    - c.___ A bunny – they're soft and cuddly
    - d.___ A teddy bear – they're good company in bed

35. Which flavor of ice cream does she like the most?
    - a.___ Vanilla
    - b.___ Chocolate
    - c.___ Coffee
    - d.___ Mint
    - e.___ Anything, as long as it's fat-free

36. Which soda does she like the most?
    - a.___ Coca-Cola
    - b.___ Pepsi
    - c.___ 7-Up
    - d.___ Dr. Pepper
    - e.___ None of the above – she prefers martinis

37. On Sunday during football season, she:
    - a.___ Watches the game with you
    - b.___ Calls her mom
    - c.___ Does her nails
    - d.___ Goes shopping

38. Which type of car does she prefer?
    - a.___ Luxury car
    - b.___ Sport-utility vehicle
    - c.___ Minivan
    - d.___ Anything convertible

Preferences

39. Which activity would she prefer to participate in?
    a.__ Jogging
    b.__ Baking
    c.__ Hiking
    d.__ Tanning

40. Which of these does she prefer to watch on television?
    a.__ Music videos
    b.__ Soap operas
    c.__ Sitcoms
    d.__ Reality TV
    e.__ Infomercials

41. Which of these dances does she prefer?
    a.__ Disco
    b.__ Salsa
    c.__ Line dancing
    d.__ Break dancing
    e.__ Dirty dancing

42. Which of these indoor activities does she prefer?
    a.__ Reading
    b.__ Watching television
    c.__ Cooking
    d.__ Decorating
    e.__ Cleaning

Shopping

43. What does she do if she finds expensive shoes she likes?
    a.__ Buys them on impulse
    b.__ Looks to see if any other store carries them at a lower price
    c.__ Waits until they go on sale
    d.__ Buys them on the Internet

44. She would rather go shopping:
    a.__ With you
    b.__ Alone
    c.__ With her friends
    d.__ With someone else's credit card

45. What is most important for her when buying clothes?
    a.__ Price
    b.__ Quality
    c.__ Style
    d.__ Whatever makes her look skinny

46. If you lose her at a mall you will most likely find her at:
    a.__ A discount store
    b.__ A specialty store
    c.__ A lingerie store
    d.__ The food court

47. What would she prefer to receive as a gift?
    a.__ A book
    b.__ A DVD
    c.__ A CD
    d.__ Flowers

Appearance

48. She would most likely get a scar from:
    a.__ Trying to rescue an injured animal
    b.__ Trying to juggle knives
    c.__ A fight with an ex-boyfriend
    d.__ Trying to walk and chew gum at the same time

49. What would she change about her appearance?
    a.__ Her eyes
    b.__ Her nose
    c.__ Her waistline
    d.__ Her butt

50. What does she like the least about herself?
    a.__ Her personality
    b.__ Her physique
    c.__ Her family
    d.__ Nothing – she's perfect

51. Which of these people would she want to look like?
    a.__ Paris Hilton
    b.__ Pamela Anderson
    c.__ Beyoncé Knowles
    d.__ Queen Latifah
    e.__ None – she just wants to make their kind of money

School Days

52. Which high school did she go to?

   _____

53. If she didn't do her homework, her excuse would be:
   a.__ The dog ate it
   b.__ There was a death in the family
   c.__ My mother threw it away by accident
   d.__ Doing homework is against my religion

54. Which class was she most likely to ditch?
   a.__ Math
   b.__ History
   c.__ Science
   d.__ English

55. Which class would she never miss at school?
   a.__ Math
   b.__ History
   c.__ Science
   d.__ English

56. She was most likely sent to the principal's office for:
   a.__ Passing love notes
   b.__ Sleeping during class
   c.__ Ditching class
   d.__ Flirting with the history teacher

57. Did she ever cheat on an exam?
   a.__ No
   b.__ Once, but she got caught
   c.__ Only when she was really desperate
   d.__ Every chance she got

Teenage Years

58. As a teenager, she was most likely known as a:
    a.___ Geek
    b.___ Preppy
    c.___ Freak
    d.___ Flirt

59. What is her favorite memory as a teenager?
    a.___ Her first car
    b.___ Her first boyfriend
    c.___ Her senior prom
    d.___ Hanging out with friends and talking about boys

60. Who was her biggest crush as a teenager?
    a.___ The captain of the football team
    b.___ The nerdy boy in science class
    c.___ The tough guy who dropped out of school
    d.___ Anyone who wore pants and smiled at her

61. As a teenager, which of these did she most likely do?
    a.___ Lie to her parents
    b.___ Shoplift
    c.___ Cheat on an exam
    d.___ Have multiple boyfriends
    e.___ All of the above

Family Matters

62. Does she love her father more than she loves you?
    a.___ Yes, she'll always be a daddy's girl
    b.___ Yes, but you're a close second
    c.___ She loves you both equally
    d.___ She loves you more but don't tell her dad

63. She thinks of her father as:
    a.___ Her best friend
    b.___ A source of wisdom
    c.___ A drill sergeant
    d.___ An alien from another planet

64. Her mother is more like:
    a.___ A talk-show host
    b.___ Betty Crocker
    c.___ The school nurse
    d.___ An undercover cop

Social Life

65. Her ideal Friday night would be spent:
    a.__ Relaxing with you at home
    b.__ Watching a fashion show on television
    c.__ Going to the movies
    d.__ Doing anything that involves drinking

66. She would rather go out with:
    a.__ A small group of friends
    b.__ A large group of friends
    c.__ Her family
    d.__ Anyone who will pick up the tab

67. She would most likely participate in:
    a.__ Group sports
    b.__ Individual sports
    c.__ Virtual sports
    d.__ Who cares about sports?

68. With her friends, she is more likely to:
    a.__ Be a couch potato
    b.__ Go shopping
    c.__ Get her nails done
    d.__ Work out

69. Her friends often try to convince her to:
    a.__ Act her age
    b.__ Get a haircut
    c.__ Get a tattoo
    d.__ Lend them some money

Situations

70. When she is frustrated, she prefers that I:
    a.__ Leave her alone
    b.__ Talk to her about the problem
    c.__ Do something to take her mind off the problem
    d.__ Buy her chocolates

71. What would she do if she got locked out of the house?
    a.__ Hang out and wait for someone to come home
    b.__ Go to the neighbor's home to ask for a phone
    c.__ Break a window and climb in
    d.__ Have a nervous breakdown

72. What would she do if she won the lottery?
    a.__ Spend the money as fast as she could
    b.__ Buy a business
    c.__ Invest in the stock market
    d.__ Share it with her friends and family

73. What would she do if she got lost?
    a.__ Stop and ask for directions
    b.__ Buy a map and figure out where she is
    c.__ Keep driving until she finds what she's looking for
    d.__ Give up and go home

74. When she retires, she will most likely:
    a.__ Play golf
    b.__ Make ceramics
    c.__ Travel
    d.__ She'll never retire – she needs the shopping money

Food and Drinks

75. Which of the following does she prefer with her chips?
    a.__ Nacho cheese
    b.__ Salsa
    c.__ Guacamole
    d.__ All the above mixed together

76. Which of these pizzas does she like the best?
    a.__ Plain cheese
    b.__ Meat lover's
    c.__ Veggie
    d.__ None of the above – she would prefer a salad

77. How does she eat an Oreo cookie?
    a.__ Sticks the whole thing in her mouth
    b.__ Dunks it in milk, then eats it
    c.__ Twists it open, licks the cream, then eats the
        two cookie halves
    d.__ Licks the cream, then puts the cookie back in
        the bag

78. How does she like her steak?
    a.__ Well-done
    b.__ Medium
    c.__ Rare
    d.__ None of the above – she'd rather eat tofu

79. Which type of food is she most likely to cook?
    a.__ American
    b.__ French
    c.__ Italian
    d.__ Anything she can heat in the microwave

Travels & Adventures

80. Her favorite place to vacation is:
    a.__ Hawaii – surf, sun and snorkeling
    b.__ Mexico – chips and margaritas
    c.__ Europe – museums, culture and art
    d.__ Her backyard – as long as she's got iced tea

81. The main reason she likes to travel is:
    a.__ Learning about other cultures
    b.__ Relaxation
    c.__ Eating exotic foods
    d.__ To get away from her family.

82. Which of these would she like to visit the most?
    a.__ The Great Wall of China
    b.__ The Egyptian pyramids
    c.__ The Grand Canyon
    d.__ Las Vegas – what happens in Vegas stays in Vegas

83. Which of these people from history would she most like to meet?
    a.__ Clark Gable
    b.__ Gandhi
    c.__ Pope John Paul II
    d.__ The Wizard of Oz

84. If she could visit any historical period, which would it be?
    a.__ Ancient Egypt – when women like Cleopatra ruled the world
    b.__ The Renaissance – for big puffy dresses
    c.__ The Sixties – peace, love and rock 'n' roll
    d.__ The Disco Era – she thinks she's Donna Summer

Daily Routine

85. Which one of these describes her the best?
    a.__ She likes to go to bed early, get up late
    b.__ She likes to go to bed early, get up early
    c.__ She likes to go to bed late, get up late
    d.__ She likes to go to bed late, get up early

86. Which home chore would she rather do?
    a.__ Wash the dishes
    b.__ Vacuum the carpet
    c.__ Do the laundry
    d.__ Take out the trash

87. What is her worst habit?
    a.__ Smoking
    b.__ Drinking
    c.__ Forgetting names
    d.__ Losing her keys

88. Which of these would she prefer to do on Sunday morning?
    a.__ Have breakfast in bed with you
    b.__ Get up and go for a run
    c.__ Get up and go shopping
    d.__ Sleep until noon

89. What would she do with an extra hour in her day?
    a.__ Exercise
    b.__ Read
    c.__ Sleep
    d.__ Work
    e.__ Spend it with you

Has She Ever

90. Has she ever broken a bone?
    Yes__ No__

91. Has she ever had multiple boyfriends at the same time?
    Yes__ No__

92. Has she ever fallen asleep while driving?
    Yes__ No__

93. Has she ever been in a car accident?
    Yes__ No__

94. Has she ever spent a night in jail?
    Yes__ No__

95. Has she ever been featured in the local newspaper?
    Yes__ No__

96. Has she ever stolen something of value?
    Yes__ No__

97. Has she ever gone skinny-dipping?
    Yes__ No__

98. Has she ever cheated in a past relationship?
    Yes__ No__

99. Has she ever been in an ambulance?
    Yes__ No__

100. Has she ever been on TV?
    Yes__ No__

Wife's Answer Sheet

Husband: Before you answer the questions in this book have your wife fill out this answer sheet. After she is finished have her remove it from this book.

1) _____

2) a.___ b.___ c.___ d.___ e.___

3) a.___ b.___ c.___ d.___ e.___

4) a.___ b.___ c.___ d.___

5) a.___ b.___ c.___ d.___

6) a.___ b.___ c.___ d.___

7) a.___ b.___ c.___ d.___ e.___

8) a.___ b.___ c.___ d.___

9) a.___ b.___ c.___ d.___

10) a.___ b.___ c.___ d.___

11) a.___ b.___ c.___ d.___

12) a.___ b.___ c.___ d.___

13) a.___ b.___ c.___ d.___

14) a.___ b.___ c.___ d.___

15) a.___ b.___ c.___ d.___

16) a.___ b.___ c.___ d.___ e.___

17) a.___ b.___ c.___ d.___

18) a.___ b.___ c.___ d.___ e.___

19) a.___ b.___ c.___ d.___

20) a.___ b.___ c.___ d.___

21) a.___ b.___ c.___ d.___

22) a.___ b.___ c.___ d.___

23) a.___ b.___ c.___ d.___ e.___

24) a.___ b.___ c.___ d.___

25) _____

26) a.___ b.___ c.___ d.___

27) a.___ b.___ c.___ d.___ e.___

28) a.___ b.___ c.___ d.___

29) a.___ b.___ c.___ d.___

30) _____

31) a.___ b.___ c.___ d.___

32) a.___ b.___ c.___ d.___

33) a.___ b.___ c.___ d.___ e.___

34) a.___ b.___ c.___ d.___

35) a.___ b.___ c.___ d.___ e.___

36) a.___ b.___ c.___ d.___ e.___

37) a.___ b.___ c.___ d.___

38) a.___ b.___ c.___ d.___

39) a.___ b.___ c.___ d.___

40) a.___ b.___ c.___ d.___ e.___

41) a.___ b.___ c.___ d.___ e.___

42) a.___ b.___ c.___ d.___ e.___

43) a.___ b.___ c.___ d.___

44) a.___ b.___ c.___ d.___

45) a.___ b.___ c.___ d.___

46) a.___ b.___ c.___ d.___

47) a.___ b.___ c.___ d.___
48) a.___ b.___ c.___ d.___
49) a.___ b.___ c.___ d.___
50) a.___ b.___ c.___ d.___
51) a.___ b.___ c.___ d.___ e.___
52) _____
53) a.___ b.___ c.___ d.___
54) a.___ b.___ c.___ d.___
55) a.___ b.___ c.___ d.___
56) a.___ b.___ c.___ d.___
57) a.___ b.___ c.___ d.___
58) a.___ b.___ c.___ d.___
59) a.___ b.___ c.___ d.___
60) a.___ b.___ c.___ d.___
61) a.___ b.___ c.___ d.___ e.___
62) a.___ b.___ c.___ d.___
63) a.___ b.___ c.___ d.___
64) a.___ b.___ c.___ d.___
65) a.___ b.___ c.___ d.___
66) a.___ b.___ c.___ d.___
67) a.___ b.___ c.___ d.___
68) a.___ b.___ c.___ d.___
69) a.___ b.___ c.___ d.___
70) a.___ b.___ c.___ d.___
71) a.___ b.___ c.___ d.___
72) a.___ b.___ c.___ d.___
73) a.___ b.___ c.___ d.___
74) a.___ b.___ c.___ d.___

75) a.___ b.___ c.___ d.___
76) a.___ b.___ c.___ d.___
77) a.___ b.___ c.___ d.___
78) a.___ b.___ c.___ d.___
79) a.___ b.___ c.___ d.___
80) a.___ b.___ c.___ d.___
81) a.___ b.___ c.___ d.___
82) a.___ b.___ c.___ d.___
83) a.___ b.___ c.___ d.___
84) a.___ b.___ c.___ d.___
85) a.___ b.___ c.___ d.___
86) a.___ b.___ c.___ d.___
87) a.___ b.___ c.___ d.___
88) a.___ b.___ c.___ d.___
89) a.___ b.___ c.___ d.___ e.___
90) yes___ no___
91) yes___ no___
92) yes___ no___
93) yes___ no___
94) yes___ no___
95) yes___ no___
96) yes___ no___
97) yes___ no___
98) yes___ no___
99) yes___ no___
100) yes___ no___